Who Was
Stephen Hawking?

Who Was Stephen Hawking?

by Jim Gigliotti

illustrated by Gregory Copeland

Penguin Workshop

For Michelle, for overcoming life's challenges and
following your dream—JG

PENGUIN WORKSHOP
An Imprint of Penguin Random House LLC, New York

Text copyright © 2019 by Jim Gigliotti.
Illustrations copyright © 2019 by Penguin Random House LLC. All rights reserved.
Published by Penguin Workshop, an imprint of Penguin Random House LLC, New York.
PENGUIN and PENGUIN WORKSHOP are trademarks of Penguin Books Ltd.
WHO HQ & Design is a registered trademark of Penguin Random House LLC.
Manufactured in China.

Visit us online at www.penguinrandomhouse.com.

Library of Congress Control Number: 2019009933

ISBN 9780451532480   10 9 8 7 6 5 4 3 2

Part of the *What Is Science & Technology?* Boxed Set, ISBN 9780593090138

Contents

Who Was Stephen Hawking?

When Stephen Hawking was a young boy, he wanted a toy train more than anything else in the world. But he lived in England in the mid-1940s, during World War II. Toy makers weren't making toys at that time. They were too busy helping the war effort. Their factories were being used to help build planes and bombs for soldiers. Toy trains were hard to come by.

So when Stephen was three years old, his father made him a wooden train. But Stephen didn't think of it as a *real* train.

He had to push it to make it go. Then Stephen's father managed to find a windup train. After he turned the key, it moved on its own, but it still wasn't the kind of train Stephen wanted.

Stephen was hoping for an electric train with real moving parts. He wanted to study how the train worked—what made it go and what made it stop. Finally, when he was old enough, he took out all the money he had in his bank account and bought himself an electric train set. That was more like it!

Stephen soon moved on to bigger things. He started building model airplanes. Then he worked on making toy boats. He didn't really care how they looked. Instead, he was more interested in how they worked. Sometimes he took things apart. He wasn't very good at putting them back together, but that didn't matter. He wanted to study how all the different parts worked with one another.

By the time he was a teenager, Stephen started thinking about how even larger things worked—really big things, like the universe, for instance. *How did it start?* he wondered. *Does it get larger? Does it get smaller? Will it ever end?*

Those are big questions! Stephen never stopped asking those big questions. Nothing could stop him. Not even a disease that kept him in a wheelchair for most of his life. Not even losing his ability to speak, and then to move at all.

Instead, he overcame the challenges of his disease and became a physicist. Physics is the study of matter (what all things are made of) and energy. People who study physics take a close look at how matter and energy move through space and time.

Stephen kept thinking about the big questions his entire adult life. He wrote articles and books about black holes, the origin of the universe, and all kinds of things. He was a famous scientist, an important thinker, and an inspiration to people all over the world.

CHAPTER 1
Beginnings

When World War II began in Europe in 1939, Frank and Isobel Hawking lived in London, England. London was heavily bombed during the war by Germany, which was fighting on the other side. Many parts of the city were destroyed.

The Hawkings' home wasn't hit, but one bomb landed just a few houses down the street from theirs.

When Isobel was pregnant with Stephen in the early 1940s, she moved for a time to Oxford,

England. It was much safer in Oxford, which is about sixty miles away. Oxford is home to the University of Oxford. There were no soldiers or important factories there, so it was not a target for the Germans.

In the safety of Oxford, Stephen Hawking was born on January 8, 1942. It was exactly three hundred years to the day after Italian physicist Galileo died. Stephen, who grew up to become a physicist, liked to joke that there was some significance to that. But he also admitted that thousands of other babies were born on that same day who didn't grow up to become famous scientists!

Frank Hawking studied medicine in college and became an expert in tropical diseases. He and Isobel lived in the Highgate section of London, where many scientists lived.

Stephen was Frank and Isobel's first child. In 1943, they had a daughter named Mary.

Galileo Galilei (1564–1642)

 Galileo Galilei is sometimes called "the father of modern physics." During his lifetime, people believed that heavier objects fell at a faster rate than lighter ones. But Galileo found that objects in motion all fall at the same rate of acceleration.

Galileo was an expert in many subjects. He was an astronomer, a mathematician, a philosopher, and an engineer.

As a Roman Catholic, he angered church leaders by arguing that the Earth orbits the sun; at the time, most people believed the sun traveled around the Earth. In 1633, he was found guilty of heresy, which means going against the teachings of the church. He spent the last nine years of his life jailed in his own home.

Another daughter, Philippa, was born in 1946. The family adopted a baby boy named Edward when Stephen was fourteen years old.

In 1950, the family moved about twenty miles north of Highgate to Saint Albans. Frank had started an important job at the National Institute of Medical Research in Mill Hill, a town outside London. It was easier for him to commute to work from there.

In Saint Albans, the Hawking family sometimes stood out from their neighbors. Eight-year-old Stephen figured it was because not as many scientists lived in Saint Albans as in Highgate. That was true, but there were probably

more things that made the Hawkings stand out.

For instance, they drove around town in an old London taxi from the years before the beginning of World War II. The kids were so embarrassed by the family car that they ducked down in the large spaces in the back seat so their friends wouldn't see them drive by! Everybody knew whose car it was, though.

The Hawking family also bought an old caravan, or horse-drawn wagon. They parked it in a field in a nearby town and used it as a vacation spot. On summer holidays, the kids slept in the caravan and the grown-ups pitched an army tent right next to it.

Life inside the Hawking house wasn't typical, either. There were books everywhere. The children even read at dinnertime.

The bookshelves—and there were many— were packed. Even when it looked like they were full, more books were shoved on top or in front of the original rows.

Not surprisingly, Stephen was somewhat quiet. He played a lot on his own. Sometimes, relatives would find him staring at the sky, thinking big thoughts.

But Stephen was not shy about expressing his opinions, and he made many friends. When his friends came over to the Hawking house, the family would put aside their books at dinnertime and talk instead. His young friends were very surprised at the grown-up topics they discussed, like religion or politics. The Hawking house, Stephen said, "was a place where my mind was constantly challenged."

CHAPTER 2
School Days

As a youngster, Stephen liked to play board games. However, games such as Monopoly quickly became too boring for his active mind. So he and a friend made up their own board games. Stephen's favorite was a war game that was very complicated. It took hours and hours to play because Stephen included so many rules.

His sister Mary later remembered that Stephen was very competitive.

He always wanted to win at whatever game he played. Draughts (say: drafts) is the English version of checkers. Stephen beat Mary at draughts every time they played—except once. When Mary finally beat him, Stephen quit playing draughts and took up chess. Mary never did beat him at that!

Although Stephen was very smart, he didn't learn to read until he was eight, and he rarely studied in school. He did not do neat work, and his handwriting was terrible. He had little interest in memorizing facts, but he had no trouble grasping concepts and ideas.

In his teenage years, Stephen and his friends built a computer. It was nothing like the laptop computers we have today. It was about the size of a refrigerator. The boys built it out of whatever spare parts they could find, including parts from old clocks.

The computer could solve only the most basic problems. But it was still the late 1950s—Stephen was way ahead of his time!

Albert Einstein

In fact, Stephen's friends called him "Einstein," after famous physicist Albert Einstein, because he was so brilliant. But Stephen was no Einstein in the classroom. Compared with the others in his grade, he was just an average student. He laughed about it later in his life: "It was, I like to think, a very bright class," he said.

Stephen was often bored in school. Physics came *too* easily for him. The solutions were obvious for someone who was thinking so far ahead. Subjects

such as chemistry were much more interesting. In chemistry, it was fun to figure out how different elements worked with one another—how some worked well, and others resulted in a bang!

Both Stephen's mother and father had gone to college at Oxford and hoped that Stephen would go there, too. But because of his average grades at Saint Albans School, there was no guarantee he would be accepted to Oxford.

There was also the question of what he would study in college. Frank Hawking wanted his son to follow in his footsteps in medicine, but Stephen had little interest in biology or in becoming a doctor. He wanted to major in math, but University College at Oxford did not offer it as a major. So Stephen settled on physics instead.

He wowed the faculty at Oxford with an impressive interview and with an even more impressive written exam for physics—nearly a perfect score! Stephen had been accepted to Oxford.

Stephen was only seventeen when he began his studies at Oxford in the fall of 1959. His classmates immediately could see that he was very

smart and really funny. Still, it took him a little
while to fit in with the other students, almost all
of whom were older—many of them by a couple
of years or more.

University of Oxford

The University of Oxford in Oxford, England, is the world's second-oldest university still in operation. (The oldest, Italy's University of Bologna, began in 1088.) There is no official date for Oxford's beginning, but it is believed to be as early as the year 1096.

Thirty-eight different colleges make up the University of Oxford. Each of the thirty-eight colleges has its own teachers and activities.

Stephen Hawking attended University College, which is the oldest of the thirty-eight.

Some of the best scholars in the world have gone to Oxford, including several dozen winners of the Nobel Prize. Many world leaders have attended the university, too, including twenty-seven prime ministers of England and one US president, Bill Clinton, who studied at University College for one year in the late 1960s before attending Yale Law School.

To be more social, Stephen joined the University College Boat Club in his second year. Although he was skinny and not very strong, he found a place among the larger rowers. He was the coxswain (sometimes shortened to *cox*), the smaller person who sits at one end of the boat to direct the rowers and steer.

It took a little while for Stephen to get the hang of being a cox. Because the river Thames is narrow at the town of Oxford, the rowing team competed in "bumping" races. In a bumping race, boats start out an equal distance from each other. They try to go fast enough to bump the boat in front and to keep from being bumped by the boat behind.

In his very first race, Stephen let go of the starting line as he was supposed to, but it got caught in the boat's rudder. (The team immediately was disqualified.) Another time, he somehow managed to direct his boat into a head-on collision with another boat. (Not his fault, he said.) Usually,

he brought the boat back in with some damage to it, or to the oars of his teammates. ("My coxing career was fairly disastrous," he admitted.)

Still, Stephen enjoyed being out on the river, with the boat speeding through the water. He made friends among the Boat Club members,

who were also impressed by how smart he was and by his sense of humor. "The rowing club also introduced me to one of my favorite pastimes at Oxford: partying!" he said.

Maybe a little too much partying. After his first year at Oxford, Stephen tended to socialize more than he studied. He later estimated that in his entire three years at University College, he spent about one thousand hours studying. That might sound like a lot, but it works out to less than one hour per day! That's actually very little studying, especially for a challenging school like Oxford, and for a difficult course of study such as physics.

Stephen skipped lectures and developed a reputation that he was difficult to work with. He once sat through a session with a tutor and then, before leaving, tore up the work they had done together and dropped it in a wastebasket!

Sometimes Stephen acted this way because he probably knew more than his tutors did. But he also thought the "cool" thing to do was to get by doing as little work as possible. Because Stephen was so smart, he got away with worse behavior than most students at the university.

CHAPTER 3
Bad News

Something was starting to concern Stephen in his final year at Oxford. Although he had always had an awkward way of walking, now he was starting to bump into things. Sometimes he stumbled unexpectedly. He had trouble tying his shoelaces. Then, one night, he fell all the way down a staircase at school. He was knocked out.

When he came to, he couldn't remember who he was or where he was. Stephen recovered from his fall, but it was a warning sign—one that he chose to ignore. He didn't let his parents know he was having problems.

Stephen's social life and his increasing clumsiness may have kept him from concentrating on his studies, but he still managed to graduate from Oxford with top honors.

A first-class degree was a requirement for Stephen's next step: working toward his doctorate at the University of Cambridge. A doctorate is a PhD, which stands for *doctor of philosophy*. It's a degree awarded in the sciences and other subjects that you work toward after college.

Stephen was only twenty years old when he entered Trinity Hall at Cambridge in the fall of 1962 to study cosmology. The cosmos is the

universe, and the word sometimes refers to the order of the universe. Cosmology is the type of physics that tries to understand the origins of our universe and the very nature of what it is made of.

Fred Hoyle

Things didn't start out great for Stephen at Cambridge. The top cosmologist there was a highly respected British scientist named Fred Hoyle. He was later knighted by the queen of England and became known as Sir Fred Hoyle. Stephen hoped to study under the famous Hoyle, but at first was disappointed to be assigned a different professor, Dennis Sciama (say: shar-ma).

Stephen's study of cosmology started off slowly, too, because it required complex math

Dennis Sciama

equations. He hadn't taken enough math courses at Oxford, and he needed to catch up. Stephen was still occasionally tripping and falling. And he was beginning to have difficulty talking normally, even sometimes slurring his speech.

After the first term at Cambridge, he went home for the Christmas break. At a 1963 New Year's party, he met a girl named Jane Wilde.

Jane, who was two years younger, already knew who Stephen was. His mother often picked up the younger Hawking children at her school. And his father had once cleaned out a swarm of bees from her family's backyard. But Stephen and Jane talked for the first time at the New Year's party. She was delighted with his wide smile, his gray eyes, and his sense of humor. One week later, they talked at length again at Stephen's twenty-first birthday party.

Not long after that party, though, Stephen found he couldn't hide his physical problems from his parents any longer, and they took him to see the family doctor. The doctor sent him to be examined at the hospital.

The doctors there poked him with needles to take muscle samples. They gave him many different tests. After two weeks, they finally gave Stephen and his family some news—and it wasn't good.

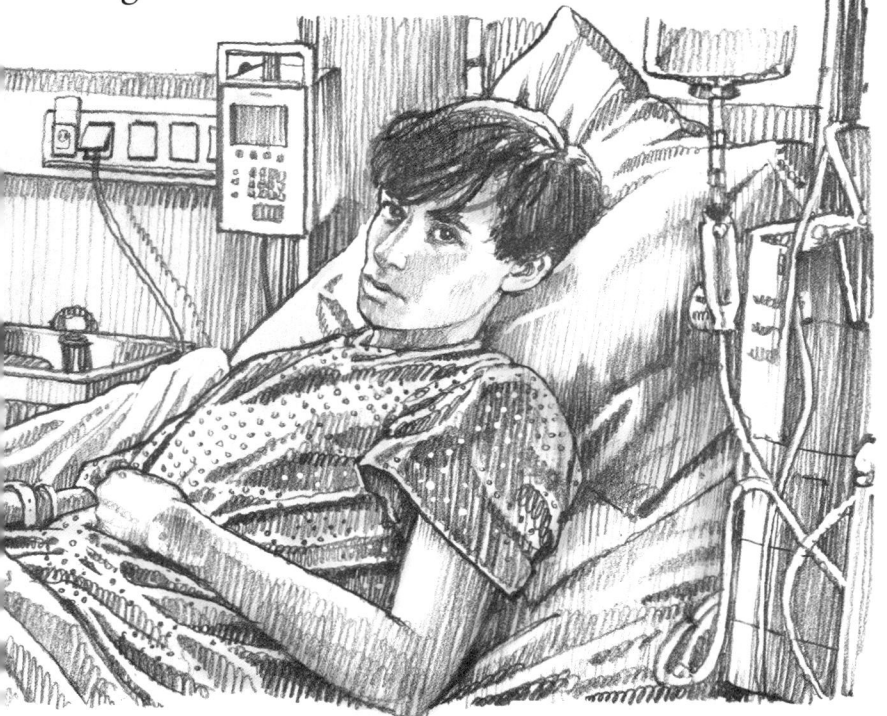

The doctors determined that Stephen had a type of disease called amyotrophic lateral sclerosis (ALS). For a patient with ALS, the cells that control the muscles of the body, called motor neurons, are affected. As the disease gets worse, a person gradually loses his or her ability to use their arms, legs, hands, and feet. They soon can't move at all, and then it becomes impossible to even breathe. ALS is an incurable disease. In the United States, it is often known as Lou Gehrig's disease, after a famous baseball player who died from it.

Stephen's doctors told him there was nothing they could do. They figured he had only about two years to live. In the meantime, they said, it was best that he go back to Cambridge. He could continue with his research there and keep working toward his doctorate degree.

Stephen took the news hard. He wasn't sure there was much point in going back to Cambridge and thinking about the big questions of the universe if he wasn't going to be around long enough to discover the answers. He hadn't felt like he was making progress even before the diagnosis.

Lou Gehrig (1903–1941)

First baseman Lou Gehrig is one of the greatest players in Major League Baseball history. In seventeen seasons with the New York Yankees, beginning in 1923, he batted .340 with 493 home runs. He earned seven All-Star Game selections, was named the American League's Most Valuable Player twice, and helped the Yankees win the World Series six times.

Gehrig was in the Yankees' lineup for every game after he became a starter in 1925. In fact, his nickname was "Iron Horse," because he played in what was then an MLB record: 2,130 games in a row! That made it all the more shocking when he was diagnosed with ALS in 1939. After a game in May of that year, he never played again.

The team honored Gehrig in a ceremony at Yankee Stadium on July 4, 1939. "For the past two weeks, you have been reading about the bad break I got," he famously told the crowd. "Yet, today, I consider myself the luckiest man on the face of the earth."

Lou Gehrig was inducted into the National Baseball Hall of Fame in 1939. He was only thirty-seven years old when he died in 1941.

Now, the disease was sure to slow him down more. He couldn't imagine even living long enough to finish his PhD, which was at least a three-year process.

Stephen was shocked and sad. He would sometimes just sit in the dark listening to classical music.

He began having terrible nightmares. His friends and his family worried about him.

Professor Sciama helped convince Stephen to return to Cambridge, and so Stephen went back to his studies. He spent some of his weekends at home. One morning, when he was on his way back to the university, he saw Jane Wilde at the train station. She was heading to London, which was along the train route to Cambridge. Jane

knew Stephen had been in the hospital, but she had not spoken to him since January.

Stephen and Jane talked on the train all the way to London, and he asked her on a date. They went to dinner and a play, and they began to see more and more of each other. They fell in love.

CHAPTER 4
Finding a Purpose

Falling in love with Jane Wilde gave Stephen, in his words, "something to live for." Like Stephen, Jane was a bit shy. And, like Stephen, she had strong opinions. She was very smart, too. She would soon be working toward her own PhD in medieval Spanish poetry.

In June, Stephen took Jane to Trinity Hall's May Ball. The May Ball is sort of like a prom in

the United States, but even fancier. And, yes: It was held in June!

Stephen and Jane had a wonderful time. Falling in love gave Stephen a reason to keep working toward his doctorate degree. If he wanted to marry Jane, he had to find a way to earn a living. And to do that, he had to finish his PhD. He started working hard for the first time in his life. "To my surprise," he said, "I found I liked it."

Much of the focus of his research was on the origin of the universe. He wanted to find out if the universe had always been essentially the same, or if it had begun with a "big bang."

Stephen was no longer disappointed that he was studying under Sciama instead of Hoyle. Sciama gave him good advice and more personal attention than Hoyle ever would have. Hoyle was often out of town giving lectures or attending conferences.

Big Bang versus Steady State

When Stephen Hawking first began working in cosmology, scientists mainly thought about the origin of the universe in two ways. They wanted to know if it came into being in a way that could be studied. Some scientists believed in the steady state theory, and some believed in the big bang theory.

According to steady state, the universe has no beginning and no end. It looks the same from any view and at any time. Even if galaxies expand and pull away from each other, new matter fills in the

spaces to keep everything pretty much the same.

According to the big bang theory, time, space, mass, and energy began from a tiny point and "exploded" to create the universe, which has been expanding ever since.

Fred Hoyle, who believed firmly in the steady state theory, came up with the name "big bang" as a way to make fun of something he thought was silly. But the name stuck. Today, most cosmologists believe in the big bang theory, while the steady state theory has little support.

Stephen applied for, and received, a research fellowship. That meant he would be getting paid to do research. He had found a job and would now have money to support a family. Stephen proposed to Jane in October of 1964, and they were married in July of 1965. They went to the

United States on their honeymoon. Jane and Stephen visited Cornell University in New York to attend a physics conference!

Stephen's ALS was quickly progressing. The good news was that he already had survived longer than the two years the doctors originally talked about. The bad news was that he needed a cane to help him walk, and he was losing strength in one arm. He couldn't even type the paper that he needed to complete his PhD. So Jane typed it for him.

Stephen received his PhD in applied mathematics and theoretical physics in March 1966. That same year, he wrote an essay that earned him a share of a major award called the Adams Prize—one of the most respected awards at Cambridge.

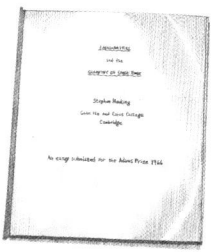

Jane continued working toward her own degree. However, most of her time was spent taking care of Stephen—and soon the couple's children. Stephen and Jane had a son named Robert, who was born in 1967. Their daughter, Lucy, was born in 1970.

Stephen continued to gradually lose the use of his hands and legs. By the late 1960s, he could not stand at a blackboard or write out long equations. He needed crutches to get around. But he resisted the idea of using a wheelchair for as long as he could. "One of the great battles was getting Stephen to use a wheelchair," Jane said. By 1969, he had no choice. He used a wheelchair for the rest of his life.

In an unexpected twist, the less mobile Stephen became and the more he had to rely on the care of others, the more time he had to think about the big questions of the universe.

CHAPTER 5
New Discoveries

One night in 1970, an idea came to Stephen in a flash just as he was getting ready for bed. Okay, maybe it wasn't really a flash. As Stephen liked to joke, it took him a long time to get ready for bed, so it gave him plenty of time to think over big questions. On this night, he was thinking about black holes, and he had a sudden realization: Some of the work he was doing could be applied to black holes.

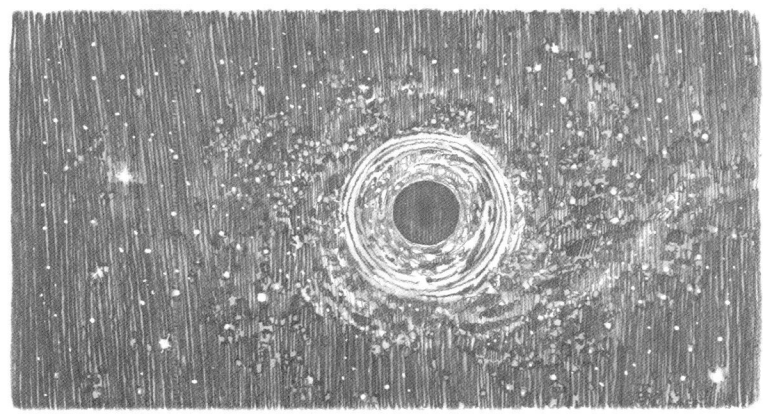

A black hole is not really black and not really a hole. It's an area in space with gravity so strong that nothing—not even light—can escape.

The boundary of a black hole is called the event horizon. Anything that crosses the event horizon is lost forever. Stephen liked the example of someone paddling in a canoe, heading toward a waterfall. If the person paddles fast and strong enough in the opposite direction, he or she can still get away from the waterfall. But once the canoe falls over the edge, it cannot go back up the waterfall.

Could energy escape the event horizon of a black hole? In 1974, Stephen found that it could—in the form of positive energy. That energy is like the person in the canoe who paddles away from the edge of the waterfall to avoid going over it. The concept eventually became known as Hawking radiation. It is perhaps the discovery Stephen is best known for.

This was a big deal because it showed that the only energy that went over the event horizon and into the black hole was negative energy, and that could shrink the hole. When the shrinking hole reached a certain point, it would explode, releasing matter back into space.

Stephen said that black holes "are not the eternal prisons they were once thought. Things can get out of a black hole, both to the outside, and, possibly, to another universe."

And then he made a joke, but one with a serious lesson: "So, if you feel you are in a black hole, don't give up. There's a way out."

Stephen may have felt as if his disease put him in his own personal black hole. But for him, the way out was through his mind. Even though his body continued to slowly break down, his mind was never affected.

 The same year Stephen discovered Hawking radiation, he worked as a visiting professor at the California Institute of Technology.

His family moved with him to Pasadena, California, for one year. Jane needed more and more help with Stephen, so they brought along a university student to help take care of him. From then on, students helped care for Stephen. That was a good situation all around: Jane got the help she needed, Stephen was cared for, and the student spent time with one of the smartest people in the world. The family returned to England in 1975, and Stephen began a job teaching and researching at Cambridge.

Stephen won several major awards and medals in the 1970s, and earned a promotion with the title of "professor" in 1977.

Then, in 1979, he became the Lucasian Professor of Mathematics at Cambridge. It might have been the most important honor of his career. There have been only nineteen Lucasian Professors—named after Henry Lucas—since England's King Charles II established the position

in 1664! Stephen was number seventeen. The most famous Lucasian Professor was Sir Isaac Newton.

In 1979, Stephen and Jane had their third child, Timothy. Stephen tried to live as normal a life as he could with his wife and children. They played in the backyard of their home, with the kids sometimes hopping into Stephen's lap for a ride on the wheelchair.

Sir Isaac Newton (1642–1727)

In 1665, twenty-two-year-old Isaac Newton sat outside his mother's farmhouse in the English countryside. He watched an apple fall from a tree, and that got him thinking. Why do objects fall to the ground? Why don't they fall up? The answer: gravity!

More than twenty years later, Newton published his three laws of motion. The first law says that if something is moving, it will keep moving until something makes it stop; if it is still, it will remain still until something makes it move. The second law uses math to show how much force is needed to make something go or stop. The third law says that "for every action, there is an equal and opposite reaction."

Newton's concepts might seem basic to us now. But in his day, they were a whole new way of thinking.

In his lifetime, Newton also made many discoveries about light, color, and math. His work on gravity and the laws of motion changed the way we think about the universe, and he is one of the most influential scientists of all time.

They went to the beach. Jane rolled Stephen's wheelchair onto the sand so the waves could splash at his bare feet.

When they weren't at the beach, Stephen developed a reputation for zipping around wildly in his wheelchair. One visitor recalls him spinning around in circles several times the moment he was first placed in the chair, then taking off with his assistant running behind, trying to catch up!

However, it was getting very difficult to understand Stephen when he talked. Often, Jane or one of Stephen's helpers had to "translate"

what he was trying to say. On November 16, 1979, Stephen signed an agreement to fulfill his duties as the Lucasian Professor of Mathematics at Cambridge. It was the last time he ever signed his name. After that, he could no longer use his hands to write. That was a problem, but he always made the best of his troubles. "One has to

be grown up enough to realize that life is not fair," he once said. "You just have to do the best you can in the situation you are in."

Because Stephen couldn't write equations about the physics of space and black holes, he had to think problems through in his mind to solve them. He relied on visualizing the way the universe worked to answer his big questions.

CHAPTER 6
A Book for Everyone

Stephen dreamed of writing a book about the answers to his big questions. But he wanted it to be a book that everyone could read and understand, not just scientists. He wanted to write a book that people could pick up at the airport, say, and read on a flight to a faraway place. After all, why should his discoveries be limited to the small group of scientists who could think like him?

Publishers weren't so sure. A book about how the universe works wasn't the kind of light reading travelers picked up at airport newsstands. It wasn't the kind of reading most people picked up at bookstores anywhere!

But Stephen really believed that people would be interested in his topic if he could explain it in everyday language. So he began working very hard at writing his book. By 1984, he had finished the first chapter, and he found a publisher who was interested. The next year, he finished writing the rest of the book.

Stephen was happy. The publisher was not. The language was still very scientific, and his theories were still too hard for most people to understand. Physics is a very complex subject! So his editor sent Stephen's manuscript back to him with suggestions for fixes.

That's not unusual in the world of publishing.

However, Stephen got sick before he could make any of the corrections. While at a conference in Switzerland, in 1985, he became very ill. An ambulance came to his hotel and rushed him to the hospital.

Stephen had pneumonia—an illness that affects the lungs and is usually treatable in healthy people. But for Stephen, who was already very sick with ALS, it looked as if it would be a disaster. Doctors gave up any hope of saving him. But Jane did not. She wanted him to return to Cambridge for treatment. The doctors warned her he could

die if they moved him. Jane insisted, and she and Stephen returned to England.

After several weeks, Stephen recovered. But in order for him to breathe on his own, without all the tubes he had been hooked up to in the hospital in Switzerland, they had to perform a surgery called a tracheotomy (say: TRAKE-ee-AH-toe-mee). After his tracheotomy, Stephen breathed only through a tube in his throat instead of through his nose and mouth. He already had trouble speaking before. Now Stephen would never be able to talk on his own again. He had no voice.

Stephen was alive, but there were new and bigger questions in his life: What would he do about work? How would he communicate with people? How could he possibly finish his book? He couldn't write it on paper. He couldn't type it himself. Now he couldn't even speak the words out loud for someone else to type. The only way he could communicate was by nodding his head or blinking when someone pointed to the letters on a spelling board. It would take forever to complete a book that way!

It was another tough time for Stephen. The many weeks of recovery "were the darkest of my life," he said. Now he needed medical care around the clock. And with nurses around all the time, there would be little privacy for Stephen and Jane.

Times may have been difficult, but Stephen and Jane never gave up hope. Britain's National Health Service and different charities agreed to help pay for Stephen's costly care. Even more valuable help came from the United States. A computer expert in California sent Stephen a program called Equalizer that would work on Stephen's computers at the university and at home. In Equalizer, Stephen could highlight

certain words or phrases by clicking a device he held in his hand. It was similar to a computer mouse. A computer-generated voice then spoke the words he had highlighted. It was a long way from today's technology, but it gave Stephen a way to communicate.

Stephen's doctors and assistants were amazed at how quickly he learned the program. The only downside was that the early versions of the software allowed him to create only about ten words per minute. That is a slow rate of speech. But, Stephen joked, "I think slowly, so it suited me quite well!"

Stephen was back in business. Although it was a long process, he finished the corrections to his manuscript. And in 1988, his book, called *A Brief History of Time*, was published around the world.

CHAPTER 7
Celebrity Status

As usual, Stephen was right. People really did want to read a book about the origins of the universe, black holes, and other scientific concepts written in everyday language. *A Brief History of Time* zoomed up the best-seller lists.

By the end of 1988, it was the top-selling nonfiction book in the United States. It also reached number one in places such as Britain, France, Germany, and Italy, and was translated into dozens of languages. It even made it into

Guinness World Records for staying more than four years on the *Sunday Times* of London best-seller list! The book is still in print today, and has sold more than ten million copies.

A Brief History of Time made Stephen an international celebrity. He was already very well-known in the scientific community, but there aren't many physicists in the world who have "celebrity" status.

Stephen was asked to give talks about his book and his career to audiences all around the world.

He was a star. He even had his own fan club!

In his office and at his home, there were many pictures of Stephen with other famous people, including Queen Elizabeth II, President Barack Obama and First Lady Michelle Obama, and three different popes: Pope John Paul II, Pope Benedict XVI, and Pope Francis.

Stephen meets Pope John Paul II.

Space Aliens

One of the photos of famous people on the wall
of Stephen Hawking's office at Cambridge shows him
with Hollywood director Steven Spielberg. Peering
between them is a space alien, the title character in
Spielberg's 1982 film *E.T.: The Extra-Terrestrial.*

With all Stephen Hawking knew about our galaxy
and the origins of the universe, what did he think
about life beyond Earth? Did he believe in aliens?
Yes! "As I grow older, I am more convinced than ever
that we are not alone," he said late in his life.

Stephen met Pope John Paul II at a gathering of scientists at the Vatican in Italy in the early 1980s. Stephen still had his voice then, although he was often difficult to understand. Pope John Paul II had to get down on one knee beside Stephen's wheelchair to get close enough to hear. "Things certainly have changed since Galileo!" another scientist at the meeting said, remembering how unfairly the church had treated that great scientist.

Unfortunately, being a celebrity wasn't always easy. It meant lots of traveling, constantly meeting with people, and giving speech after speech. Stephen began spending less time with his family. He and Jane drifted apart. They separated in 1990 and officially divorced in 1995.

That same year, Stephen married Elaine Mason. She had been one of the nurses who took care of him. Stephen and Elaine were married for eleven years before divorcing in 2006.

The Chair

Stephen's first wheelchair in 1969 was very basic. But in his later years, he used a chair that was a high-tech marvel.

From his chair, Stephen could write speeches, send e-mails, and browse the web. He could talk to visitors and communicate over Skype. He could

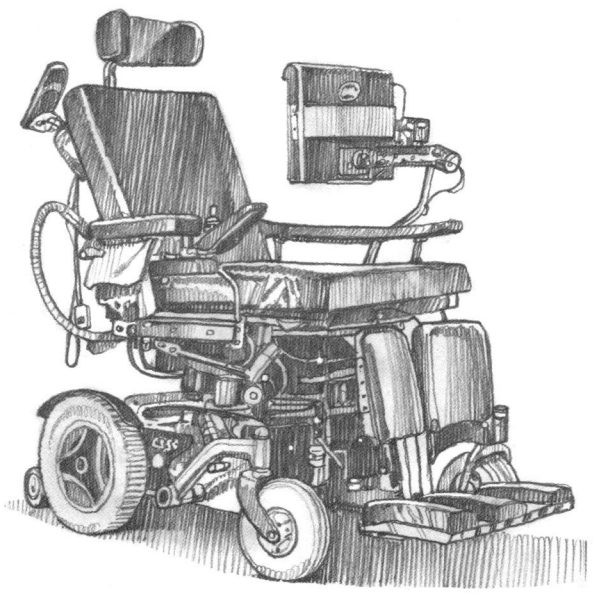

even operate the TV, turn the lights on and off, and open and close doors. It was all done with a sensor attached to his glasses. The sensor controlled a computer system mounted on the arm of his chair.

The computer was a Windows tablet PC with a twelve-inch screen. The sensor on his glasses detected movement in the cheek muscle Stephen twitched to highlight letters, words, phrases, or commands. Written words were translated into Stephen's "voice" by a synthesizer—an electronic instrument that produces sound—mounted on the back of the chair. Everything was powered by a battery pack kept under the seat.

CHAPTER 8
The Human Spirit

By the 1990s, Stephen was famous around the world. He was, of course, instantly recognizable because he was never out of his wheelchair, and he was one of the smartest people on the planet. And his fame was still growing.

In 1991, *A Brief History of Time* was made into a movie. Although it had the same title as Stephen's best-selling book, it was mostly about his life.

At one showing of *A Brief History of Time*, the actor Leonard Nimoy introduced Stephen to the people watching. Nimoy had played the character Spock in the science-fiction television show *Star Trek* and several *Star Trek* movies. When he found out that Stephen was a big fan of the show, he helped get Stephen invited to the set of *Star Trek: The Next Generation*. And when the makers of the show asked him to appear on an episode, Stephen said yes.

Leonard Nimoy

After that, Stephen was often asked to appear as a guest on TV shows. In 1999, he first showed up (in animated form, of course) on *The Simpsons* in an episode called "They Saved Lisa's Brain."

"Descent"

Q: Who is the only guest star to appear as himself
or herself on an episode of any *Star Trek* series?

A: Stephen Hawking!

In a 1993 episode of *Star Trek: The Next Generation* called "Descent," Stephen traveled to the twenty-fourth century to play a game of poker with fellow physicists Sir Isaac Newton and Albert Einstein, as well as *Star Trek*'s own character Data.

At the end of the game, Einstein was certain he had won. However, Stephen revealed his cards to show he had the winning hand. "Wrong again, Albert!" Stephen said with a large grin on his face. Stephen still loved being right!

Stephen went on to perform in several more episodes of *The Simpsons*, and also on *Futurama*. He made seven appearances in the television comedy *The Big Bang Theory*, sometimes only in voice.

Stephen with the cast of *The Big Bang Theory*

Stephen's voice was very distinctive. It was a little robotic, but with enough rise and fall and tone to make it sound human, too. But it also sounded American! Stephen was born in England, but, remember, the original software was sent by a computer expert in the United States. Eventually, technology allowed Stephen to change his computer's voice. But he didn't want to. It had become part of who he was.

Because he had had ALS for more than half a century, Stephen's body was completely disabled. His muscles no longer worked. He was totally reliant on the care of others. He was fed and cleaned and dressed and bathed by helpers. He needed someone to push his wheelchair. By 2008, he couldn't even use his hand to click the mouse on his computer.

But while his voice may have sounded a bit out of date compared with more modern technology, the software that allowed Stephen to communicate sure wasn't. Over the final ten years of his life, Stephen "spoke" by using a single cheek muscle to move the cursor on his computer. The advanced software used text recognition,

sort of like the technology on a smartphone. It also allowed Stephen to open programs such as e-mail, Microsoft Word, and Skype.

What would have happened if one day Stephen could no longer move that cheek muscle? It was a real concern. Scientists began working with him on facial recognition software, and even on trying to convert brain signals into speech. This conversion is called brain-machine interface, or BMI. Stephen experimented with BMI, but made very little progress. Although it did not happen in Stephen's lifetime, scientists hope to translate brain signals into speech in the near future.

"Because each new day could be my last," Stephen once said, "I have developed a desire to make the most of each and every minute." He did that by maintaining an active life despite his disease.

In 2007, he experienced weightlessness on

NASA's zero-gravity aircraft. With the help of NASA experts, he floated, rose, dipped, and was even spun around. The grin on his face gave away what a good time he had.

That same year, Stephen and his daughter, Lucy, wrote a children's book. *George's Secret Key to the Universe* featured a computer called Cosmos that helps people travel into outer space. Four other books in the series followed.

In 2009, President Barack Obama presented Stephen with the Presidential Medal of Freedom for his contributions to science. It's the highest US honor awarded to civilians.

In 2012, Stephen helped launch the Paralympic Games in London with a speech at the opening ceremony. "The Paralympic Games are all about transforming our perception of the world," he told the competitors and the spectators at London's

Olympic Stadium. "We are all different. There is no such thing as a standard or run-of-the-mill human being, but we share the same human spirit. However difficult life may seem, there is always something you can do and succeed at."

Stephen's life was incredibly difficult, but he never lost his intense desire to succeed.

In 2014, the love story of Stephen and Jane Wilde was made into the movie *The Theory of Everything*.

Stephen poses with the two stars of *The Theory of Everything*.

Eddie Redmayne played Stephen, and Felicity Jones played Jane. Near the end of the movie, Stephen's character tells Jane's character, "Look what we've made." He meant the family they built, but also the many other successes along the way.

On March 14, 2018, Stephen died peacefully in his sleep at home in Cambridge. He was seventy-six. It had been more than fifty years since doctors predicted he wouldn't live beyond age twenty-three. Until his death, he was actively working at Cambridge as Director of Research at the Centre for Theoretical Cosmology.

What was Stephen Hawking's most important accomplishment? Was it his scientific discoveries, such as Hawking radiation? Was it his heroic personal journey, never letting his disease keep him from living life to its fullest? Or was it explaining difficult scientific ideas to people all over the world through his best-selling book?

Stephen Hawking's life was full of big questions. And throughout it, he worked tirelessly to come up with the right answers.

Timeline of Stephen Hawking's Life

1942	Stephen Hawking is born on January 8 in Oxford, England
1959	Enters University College, Oxford
1963	Is diagnosed with motor neuron disease ALS (Lou Gehrig's disease)
1965	Marries Jane Wilde
1966	Completes his PhD at the University of Cambridge
1967	Son Robert is born
1970	Daughter, Lucy, is born
1974	Discovers what is now known as "Hawking radiation"
1979	Becomes the Lucasian Professor of Mathematics at the University of Cambridge
	Son Timothy is born
1988	*A Brief History of Time* is published
1991	*A Brief History of Time*, a documentary film about Stephen and his life, is released
1995	Divorces Jane Wilde and marries Elaine Mason
2006	Divorces Elaine Mason
2009	Is awarded the Presidential Medal of Freedom, the United States' highest civilian honor
2012	Officially opens the Paralympic Games in London
2014	*The Theory of Everything*, a movie about Stephen and Jane's love story, is released
2018	Dies on March 14 in Cambridge, England

Timeline of the World

1939 — Germany invades Poland, and World War II begins

1945 — In August, atomic bombs are dropped on the Japanese cities Hiroshima and Nagasaki by the United States, leading to the end of World War II

1951 — The first color TV is sold

1955 — Rosa Parks is arrested in Montgomery, Alabama, for refusing to give up her seat on a bus to a white passenger

1961 — In April, Soviet cosmonaut Yuri Gagarin becomes the first person to travel into space; in May, US astronaut Alan B. Shepard Jr. becomes the first American in space

1969 — American Neil Armstrong becomes the first person to walk on the moon

1976 — Steve Jobs, Steve Wozniak, and Ronald Wayne start Apple Computer Inc.

1997 — The first Harry Potter novel is published in the United Kingdom

2001 — On September 11, terrorist attacks in the United States destroy the World Trade Center in New York City and kill almost three thousand people

2008 — Barack Obama is elected the first African American president of the United States

2018 — Privately owned company SpaceX launches its Falcon Heavy rocket into space

Bibliography

*Books for young readers

*Fortey, Jacqueline. *Great Scientists.* New York: DK Publishing, 2007.

Hawking, Jane. *Travelling to Infinity: My Life with Stephen.* London: Alma Books, 2007.

*Hawking, Lucy, and Stephen Hawking. *George's Secret Key to the Universe.* New York: Simon & Schuster Books for Young Readers, 2007.

Hawking, Stephen. *My Brief History.* New York: Bantam Books, 2013.

Hawking, Stephen W. *The Illustrated Theory of Everything: The Origin and Fate of the Universe.* Beverly Hills, CA: Phoenix Books, 2003.

*Senker, Cath. *Stephen Hawking.* Chicago: Heinemann-Raintree, 2016.

White, Michael, and John Gribbin. *Stephen Hawking: A Life in Science.* New York: Dutton, 1992.